Butterflies For Kids
Amazing Animal Books For Young Readers

By Valeria Arcas
Mendon Cottage books

JD-Biz Publishing

Download Free Books!
http://MendonCottageBooks.com

Read More Amazing Animal Books

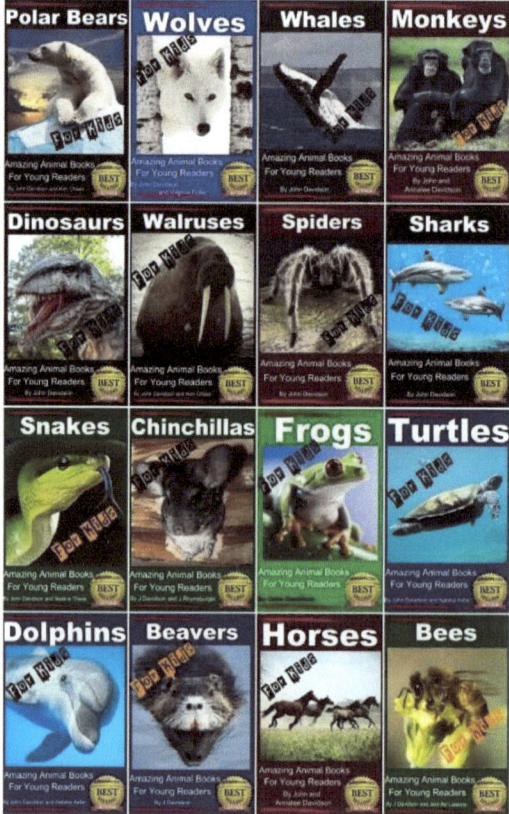

Download Free Books!
http://MendonCottageBooks.com

Table of Contents

Introduction

Have you ever seen a green caterpillar? Needless to say, it is not a very pretty insect. Have you ever seen a butterfly? I can guess the answer is yes; butterflies are beautiful. Did you know that caterpillars turn into butterflies? How is it possible that an ugly insect turns into such a beauty! Together we will discover the surprising life cycle of a butterfly. Butterflies are very important for the ecosystems, and here you will learn about butterflies and their jobs as pollinators. Did you know that butterflies fly thousands of miles from one country to another? That is a very long journey! How long does a butterfly live? How many species of butterflies exist? There are thousands of them, all different in color and size. We are going to find the answers to these and more questions.

Butterflies Beautiful Insects

There are thousands of insects in the world, but there is no doubt that butterflies are some of the most beautiful insects on the planet. Butterflies are admired for their beauty. Their scientific name is **Papilionoidea** and belongs to the group of **Lepidoptera**, which means "scaly wings".

In some cultures butterflies are symbols of rebirth because they emerge and grow into something beautiful. Butterfly watching is a popular hobby for many people that like to discover different species.

Like all insects they have: a head, thorax, abdomen (three body parts), two antennae and six legs. Butterflies also have four wings covered by colored scales; pigments produce most of the colors. It is not good when people touch butterflies wings; the powder that comes off is actually scales, so their wings get damaged.

There are butterflies in different colors and sizes, some of them are very small less than one inch (1 in.), and some others reach eleven inches (11 in.) with their wings spread. They make a big contribution to the ecosystem doing pollination. There are about 18,000 species of butterflies around the world, and 450 species in North America.

Fossils found have shown that butterflies have been on the planet for at least 130 million years. The largest butterfly known on Earth is Queen Alexandra's Birdwing which has a wingspan of 31 cm. and is found in New Guinea. The smallest one is the Western Pigmy Blue which is very hard to spot and it lives in The United States, Mexico and South America

The life span of a butterfly is very short; it is about a month. Some species like Monarchs, Mourning Cloaks and Tropical Heliconians can live up to nine months.

Anatomy of a Butterfly

Butterflies are insects, and like all insects they have three body parts and legs but they also have some other body parts, let's learn about them!

The life of a butterfly begins as an egg, then a caterpillar, followed by a chrysalis and finally a butterfly. When the butterfly emerges from the chrysalis, and its body has changed, it has the same basic parts but it also develops new ones. The head, thorax and abdomen are still there, now there is also a proboscis (a large tube) and 4 wings.

Head: Sensory organs are on the head like the antennae and the eyes. They also have the proboscis and the brain there.

Compound Eyes: These are formed by many hexagonal lenses, detect color and movement, and send the information to the brain.

Antennae: Detect smells and sense butterfly's position. Butterflies smell with their antennae!

Labial Palps: Are hair-covered organs that help the butterfly to decide whether or not something is food.

Abdomen: The butterfly's abdomen is divided into 10 tiny segments. It holds the heart, the digestive system, reproductive organs and spiracles (breathing holes).

Thorax: Divided in three segments and holds the moving parts of the butterfly, wings and legs.

Legs: Six legs are attached to the thorax. The front pair of legs is used to clean the antennae. Legs are taste organs they have diminutive grasping claws to taste food.

Wings: Butterfly's wings are extremely thin made of a material called chitin (tiny scales). Wings have lots of veins that bring oxygen and blood to them. The forewings are closer to the head and the hind wings are closer to the tail.

Life Cycle of a Butterfly

The life cycle of butterflies is an amazing process in which a caterpillar turns into a beautiful butterfly. It takes four different stages that begins with the eggs and ends with the butterflies. This changing process is named **metamorphosis.**

First stage: An adult female lays eggs on a plant. The butterfly "glues" the eggs to the leaf with a sticky liquid. The eggs are very small and round; the butterfly lays them together. It takes about five days for the eggs to begin hatching. A tiny green worm hatches from the eggs.

Second stage: The baby caterpillars crawl and the first thing they do is eat the eggshell. Once they finish it, they start eating leaves where they were laid and then the leaves around them. This is the stage where the caterpillar eats more; they are like munching machines. In this stage the caterpillars grow very fast. The caterpillars have a striped or patched pattern. When the caterpillars grow and get too big for their covering, they shed their skin and grow a new one. The caterpillars shed its skin about five times.

Third stage: A fully-grown caterpillar attaches itself to a twig or a leaf and forms a hard skin known as **chrysalis or pupa.** The pupa can be green or brown and it camouflages with the leaves or branches around it, so it cannot get hurt. In this stage the caterpillar stops growing. This stage is for resting. The caterpillar stays in the cocoon for two weeks.

Fourth stage: The chrysalis opens, an adult butterfly emerges with its wings folded against its body, and they are wet and soft. At this moment the butterfly cannot fly, it needs to wait for a couple of hours while its wings dry and fill with blood. Then the butterfly learns how to fly fast. Now the butterfly flies looking for food and for a mate.

The whole metamorphosis process from an egg to a butterfly can last up to a year.

Butterflies Habitat

There is no specific place where butterflies live. We can find butterflies in almost every part of the world. The only place where butterflies are not found is in Antarctica or in very dry deserts where there is no food for them. Their habitats include everything from tropical forests to grasslands to tundra, wetlands and alpine. Warm weather is best for them and a large amount of butterflies live in the tropics. Places like California, Hawaii and Mexico are some of butterflies' favorites.

Butterflies are constantly moving from one place to another, and they are always looking for food. During the day butterflies are active; they can sense climate changes, so they know when it is going to rain and they hide under leaves or in trees trunks. At night the butterflies rest on the underside of leaves or between rocks.

Some butterflies live at the top of tall trees and don't fly to the ground. But, what happen during winter? If butterflies cannot fly when they are cold, how do they survive during winter? There are some different answers for this question: Most butterflies don't spend winters as butterflies; they spend it as caterpillars eating and growing. Caterpillars are more resilient than butterflies. Some spend the winter as a chrysalis, other adult butterflies can hibernate in holes of trunks and the last option is to migrate. Some butterflies species like, the Monarch, migrate to a warmer place.

What Do Butterflies Eat?

Butterflies don't eat like humans or other animals; butterflies get their food from drinking. They don't have a mouth like us; instead they have a little narrow pipe that acts like a straw (proboscis). The butterfly sits on top of a flower and drinks the nectar.
Butterflies have six feet; these feet have sensors that help them to taste things.

Butterflies don't eat only nectar; they can eat some other things like pollen, rotting fruit, dung or tree sap, and mineral rocks. But all their food needs to be in liquid state. Butterflies have an excellent sense of smell, which allows them to find food.

A big difference between butterflies and caterpillars is when they are caterpillars they eat lots of leaves, all day and night.

Can Butterflies Communicate?

Butterflies can communicate among each other, between the same species, or even different species. They can communicate by their color, sound, physical actions, and by chemicals that are released.

Some butterflies make clicking sounds to protect their space. Male butterflies use aggressive postures in courtship. Color patterns help them to distinguish males from females.

Butterflies cannot hear, so, they feel vibrations. There is a butterfly named Cracker Butterfly, and it can produce loud sounds with its wings.

Butterflies and Pollination

It is always pleasant to watch a garden full of beautiful flowers and butterflies. Colorful flowers attract butterflies as well as the scent; they can see bright colors such as red, green and yellow. It is true that butterflies are not as good of pollinators as bees, but they do a great job too. Butterflies pollinate a wide variety of flowers; they walk around flower clusters and gather pollen that sticks to their tiny legs.

At the same time they are looking for food, they help plants reproduce. Butterflies have an advantage over bees as they can travel longer distances.

Butterflies and plants depend on each other. Flower plants provide the butterfly with food, nectar, and pollen. Butterflies lay eggs on a host plant. Leaves provide camouflage to the pupa while the caterpillar is transforming. In return, butterflies help flowering plants to reproduce. Each butterfly species has a particular host plant and that is why it is important to preserve their ecosystem. They also have a particular nectar plant to pollinate.

Monarch Butterfly and Migration

Monarch butterflies are probably the most famous butterflies of all. They are very colorful: orange, white and black. This coloring actually sends a warning to predators that they are poisonous. When caterpillars, monarch butterflies eat milkweed plant leaves which actually contain a poisonous toxin that is stored in their bodies. That is why monarch butterflies taste awful to their predators.

Males are bigger than females; they also have a black dot along the veins of their wings. A Monarch butterflies average wingspan is 9.3 cm to 10.5 cm.

A female Monarch can lay 400 eggs. They are always depositing them on milkweed leaves. Striped caterpillars hatch from the eggs.

Monarch butterflies have four generations through the year:

First Generation is born during March and April. This generation lasts from 2 to 6 weeks.

Second Generation is born between May and June. This generation lasts from 2 to 6 weeks.

Third Generation is born during July and August. This generation lasts from 2 to 6 weeks.

Fourth Generation is born between September and October. This generation doesn't die and they last for about a year. This is the generation that migrates.

Monarch butterflies don't survive in cold weather. In winter, they begin a fantastic journey; they migrate from United States to Mexico (some of them stay in California), where they will be warmer and will have enough food to survive. Migration starts in October and they spend all winter in Mexico.

Monarch butterflies are the only butterfly species that fly 3,000 miles, and this is why they are so famous and appealing to people. Every year hundreds of people gather to see them in their sanctuaries.

During migration, thousands of Monarch butterflies will land on a single tree. Monarch butterflies are protected, as well as, their ecosystem; people cannot touch them or be near of them.

Butterfly Species

There are about 18,000 butterfly species around the world. The country with most different species is Peru. We are going to mention only a few of them, the most commonly known.

Painted Lady Butterfly: This butterfly is well known around the world. It lives in North and South America, Europe, Asia and Africa. It prefers tropical areas with lots of trees. As caterpillar it eats daisy flowers and cloves leaves, and when it becomes a butterfly it prefers clover nectar. The Painted Lady Butterfly is mostly black, brown and orange with some white spots. Its wingspan is 5.1 cm to 7.3 cm. These butterflies live for about two weeks.

Viceroy Butterfly: It is found in United States, Canada and Mexico. The Viceroy caterpillar is white and brown in color. It eats leaves of willow and poplar trees. The Viceroy Butterfly is dark orange with black veins and a row of white spots on the edge of the wings. This butterfly tries to mimic the Monarch Butterfly with the same colors and wing pattern.

Buckeye One Butterfly: This is one of the most distinctive butterflies in North America, and it is also found in Mexico. It chooses gardens, parks, fields, and agricultural lands for its habitat. The Buckeye One caterpillar is black with white and orange stripes; it likes to eat monkey flower, snapdragon, and plantain. Buckeye One Butterfly is brown with two orange cells and big eyespots. The wingspan is 4.5 cm to 7.0 cm. Females are bigger than males.

Zebra Longwing Butterfly: Lives in tropical areas of southern North America, West Indies, Central and South America. It is black with bold narrow yellow stripes and several red spots. It camouflages well from predators and has a bad taste for them. The Zebra Longwing wingspan is 7.2 cm to 10 cm. This butterfly loves to eat sweet nectar from lantana and it makes a loud cricking sound when it is in danger.

Now let's mention some more exotic butterfly species:

Paper Kite Butterfly: Also called **Rice Paper Butterfly**, found in West Malaysia, Taiwan and Philippines. They live in tropical rainforests. The chrysalis is yellow with black markings and the butterfly is black and white (it really looks made from paper!) Its wingspan is 9.5 cm to 11 cm.

Tailed Jay Butterfly: It is a black butterfly with many green spots; its wingspan is 8 cm to 9 cm. The Tailed Jay Butterfly belongs to the family of the Swallowtail Butterfly. They can be found in India, Sri Lanka, Southeast Asia and Australia.

Mexican Bluewing Butterfly: Its name is Mexican but it lives in Colombia, Central America and of course Mexico. They like to live in tropical forests and open valleys. The Mexican Bluewing Butterfly is black with blue iridescent bands and some white spots in the outer part of the wing. Its wingspan is 6.4 cm to 7.6 cm. These butterflies enjoy eating the juices of rotting fruit.

Doris Longwing Butterfly: These gorgeous butterflies come in different colors. The background is black and the patch of color can be red, blue, orange or dark cream. They are found in regions from Central America to the Amazon Rainforest. Its wingspan is 7.5 cm to 8.3 cm. The Doris Longwing Butterfly lives up to 9 months and it can ingest pollen as well as nectar.

Butterfly Meaning in Different Cultures

Butterflies have had a significant importance during ancient times to present. They represent different things and have different meanings in cultures around the world.

- Ancient Romans believed butterflies were broken flowers.

- In Japan, butterflies represent happiness and joy. To see a butterfly in a Japanese house is sign of good luck.

- In Germany, they believe that dead are reborn as children who fly as butterflies.

- Mexican tribes see butterflies as a symbol of fertility.

- In Ireland people believe that butterflies are souls waiting to pass through the purgatory.

- Greeks believed a new human soul was born each time a butterfly emerged from the chrysalis.

- In Chinese culture, seeing two butterflies flying together symbolizes love and long life.

Butterfly Facts

There are some interesting facts about butterflies that we have not discovered yet:

- The fastest butterfly is the Skipper Butterfly. It can fly at 37 miles per hour. The average speed is 5 to 12 miles per hour. (Wow it is fast!)

- Butterflies are cold-blooded animals. They need sun to fly.

- A butterfly can see ultraviolet colors that humans cannot see.

- A group of butterflies is called a "Flutter"

- Butterflies are the second group of pollinators. Bees are the first.

- In Pacific Groove California there is a butterfly themed parade.

- Butterflies largest threat is habitat's loss.

-Butterflies cannot hear, just feel vibrations.

Conclusion

This has been an incredible learning journey through a butterflies' life. We have discovered what amazing creatures these are. They are born from an egg and develop into beautiful butterflies, their importance for the planet as pollinators and why they migrate to warmer places.

There are many places where you can go to watch butterflies and learn more about them. Ask your parents to take you now that you have read this incredible book of these amazing animals!

Author Bio

Born in Mexico City, since a child I always loved English language, when college time arrived my decision was clear and I majored in English Language but, I also like kids, teaching, and writing. I have been a teacher for 20 years. The last few years I decided to write a children's book, then another one came and I'm on the road, it has been a great experience.

Our books are available at
1. Amazon.com

2. Barnes and Noble

3. Itunes

4. Kobo

5. Smashwords

6. Google Play Books

Download Free Books!
http://MendonCottageBooks.com

Publisher

JD-Biz Corp

P O Box 374

Mendon, Utah 84325

http://www.jd-biz.com/

www.ingramcontent.com/pod-product-compliance
Lightning Source LLC
Chambersburg PA
CBHW050907290526
45792CB00002B/721